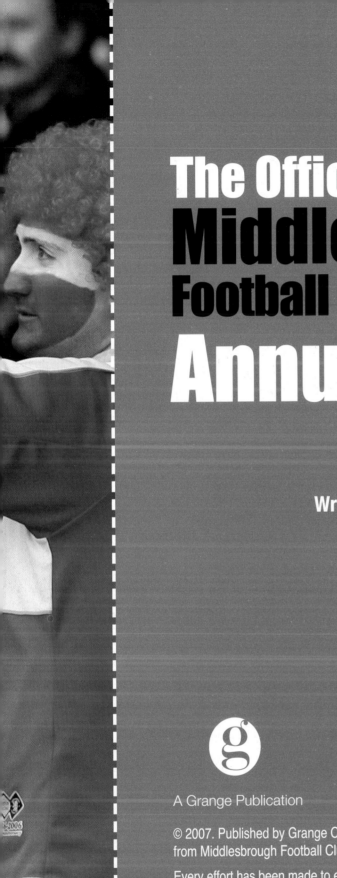

C000180565

The Official Middlesbrough Football Club Annual 2008

Written By Dave Byrne

g

A Grange Publication

© 2007. Published by Grange Communications Ltd., Edinburgh, under licence from Middlesbrough Football Club. Printed in the EU.

Every effort has been made to ensure the accuracy of information within this publication but the publishers cannot be held responsible for any errors or omissions. Views expressed are those of the author and do not necessarily represent those of the publishers or the football club. All rights reserved.

ISBN 978-1-905426-88-1

Photographs courtesy of Middlesbrough Football Club, BladesSport Photography, Highland Studios and Getty Images. MFC logo and crest are registered trademarks of the Middlesbrough Football Club.

£6.99

Contents

All About Gareth

Here's the facts about Boro manager Gareth Southgate

- Gareth was former manager Steve McClaren's first signing for Boro in the summer of 2001.

- Boro paid Aston Villa £6.5 million for Southgate. That makes him the fifth most expensive Boro player ever behind Jonathan Woodgate (£7 million), Yakubu (£7.5 million), Ugo Ehiogu (£8 million) and Massimo Maccarone (£8.15 million).

- Gareth was not Boro's captain for his first season at the Riverside. His former England team-mate Paul Ince remained Boro captain until he left the club in 2002.

- Boro fans voted Southgate the club's greatest ever captain in a poll on the club's official website at www.mfc.co.uk.

- Southgate was the first ever Boro captain to lift major silverware when leading the club to victory in the Carling Cup final against Bolton on February 29 2004.

- Gareth began his career as a midfielder at Crystal Palace before becoming one of the best central defenders in the country.

- He did not make his first team debut for Crystal Palace until he was 20. He played over 100 appearances for Palace reserves.

- He went on to play 57 times for England, including a win over Slovakia at the Riverside Stadium in June 2003.

- In the summer of 2007, a year after retiring from playing, Southgate remained fifth in the all-time list of Premier League appearances behind only Gary Speed, David James, Ryan Giggs and Alan Shearer.

- In all he made more than 500 league appearances for Crystal Palace, Aston Villa and Boro.

- Gareth Southgate became manager of Boro in May 2006 after Steve McClaren took charge of the England team.

- His first match as Boro manager ended in a 3-2 defeat at Reading, but his first home game as boss was a fantastic 2-1 win over Chelsea.

- When he was a young boy Gareth's football hero was Manchester United and England legend Bryan Robson, who has also been Boro manager.

HISTORY LESSON
Your Boro factfile and club records

Year formed
1876

Year re-formed
1986

Honours
Carling Cup winners, 2004

UEFA Cup runners-up, 2006

Coca-Cola Cup runners-up, 1997, 1998

FA Cup runners-up, 1997

Division One champions, 1995

Division Two champions, 1927, 1929, 1974

Anglo-Scottish Cup winners, 1975

Zenith Data Systems Cup runners-up, 1990

FA Amateur Cup winners, 1895, 1898

Record defeat
0-9 v Blackburn, Division Two, November 6 1954

Record league win
9-0 v Brighton, Division Two, August 23 1958

8-0 v Huddersfield, Division One, September 1950

8-0 v Sheffield Wednesday, Division Two, April 1973

Record cup wins
11-0 v Scarborough, FA Cup qualifying match, October 1890

8-0 v Willington Athletic, FA Cup qualifying match, November 1900

7-0 v Hereford, Coca-Cola Cup 2nd round, September 18 1996

Record transfer fees

£8.15 million	Massimo Maccarone	July 2002
£8 million	Ugo Ehiogu	October 2000
£7.5 million	Yakubu	July 2005
£7 million	Fabrizio Ravanelli	July 1996
£7 million	Jonathan Woodgate	July 2007

Highest league scorers

George Camsell	325
George Elliott	203
Brian Clough	197
John Hickton	159
Micky Fenton	147

Most league appearances

Tim Williamson	563
Gordon Jones	462
Jacky Carr	421
George Camsell	418
John Hickton	415

QUIZ 1:
The Players

Answers on page 61

1. From which club did Boro sign Jonathan Woodgate for £7 million?

2. In what country was George Boateng born?

3. Who became Boro's most expensive ever signing for £8.15 million?
   Was it (a) Mark Viduka (b) Ugo Ehiogu (c) Massimo Maccarone

4. Which young Boro player scored on his first team debut in a 4-3 FA Cup win against Hull City in January 2007?

5. Which club did Ugo Ehiogu join when he left the Riverside in January 2007?

6. Who was Boro's top scorer with 19 goals in the 2006-07 season?

7. Who scored once and set up three goals when Boro beat Bolton 5-1 in January 2007?

8. Which Boro player made his League debut while on loan to Bradford City?

9. What is the name of the defender who joined Boro from Bayer Leverkusen in the summer of 2005?

10. True or false: Jonathan Woodgate made his England comeback against Spain?

Meet the Backroom Boys!

Come behind the scenes to take a look at Gareth Southgate's backroom boys – discover that behind the great man is a great team of staff...

THE COACHES

It has been an incredibly busy time for Gareth Southgate since he became Boro manager during the summer of 2006 – and he couldn't have done so well if he didn't have such a fantastic group of coaches working for him.

When former Boro star Colin Cooper hung up his boots to concentrate on coaching he joined a great team of unsung heroes who assist the manager with all the coaching and tactics every day at Boro's Rockliffe Park training ground – and, of course, on matchdays at the Riverside.

These include first team coach Steve Harrison, reserve team coach Steve Agnew and under-18s coach Martin Scott.

Colin Cooper

THE GOALKEEPER COACHES

Former Arsenal and Crystal Palace goalkeeper Paul Barron is the man who ensures that all of Boro goalkeepers are on top form whenever they play either for Boro's first team or reserves.

Working with Boro legend Stephen Pears, Barron gives specialist goalkeeper coaching to the first team 'keepers plus those coming through the ranks – such as talented young England stars like Ross Turnbull and Jason Steele.

THE PHYSIOS

Boro's Medical Department is headed by Grant Downie, who joined Boro from Scottish giants Rangers. Grant and his team are in charge of all of the players' medical problems and ailments, from broken legs to sore throats!

With so many players based at the training ground every day, there's always a few players who need either long-term injuries or slight bruises or knocks treating. That's where Grant and physio assistant Nick Allamby come in. Nick has often worked closely with Jonathan Woodgate to ensure the England defender remains fit and ready to play.

And senior physio Chris Moseley is the man you see running onto the pitch whenever a Boro player is injured during a game. Chris is always first on the scene to give them urgent treatment or advice to ensure they are quickly back on their feet.

THE SPORTS SCIENTISTS

Premier League football isn't only about skill and tactics. It's about fitness too. And Boro have their own sports science department dedicated to making sure that each player is getting the very best from his body, ensuring they can go the extra mile when the pressure is on.

The head of sports science is Chris Barnes, who once worked at the University of Teesside, and he is assisted by a top quality team including Peter Hood.

THE MASSEUR

Many of the Boro players love a massage to loosen them up and ensure their muscles are supple and ready for the heat of a Premier League battle. Others love a massage after the match to help them relax and sooth away all those bumps and bruises!

That's when they call on Dave French, a former policeman who is now Boro's main man for massage.

THE DOCTOR

You just never know when one of the Boro players are going to feel unwell – and it's important they start feeling better as soon as possible when Premier League points are at stake.

So Boro have their very own doctor on hand in the form of Dr Brian Blacklidge, who calls in at Rockliffe Park regularly from his own medical practice in Stokesley.

THE DIETICIAN

You are what you eat – or so the saying goes! And eating healthily is absolutely crucial for sportsmen like Boro's Premier League stars.

Claire Harrison is responsible for advising each of the players on the best diets.

THE ACADEMY MEN

While Boro's first team stars get all the glory, Middlesbrough are famous for bringing so many local boys through from the club's youth squad. In fact, Boro's Academy is seen by many as the best in the country.

In charge of the Academy is former England schoolboys coach David Parnaby – father of former Boro star Stuart (now with Birmingham) – while he is assisted by experienced Ron Bone, who is in charge of a team of scouts watching local junior leagues for the next Stewart Downing, Lee Cattermole or Andrew Taylor!

Chris Barnes

Paul Barron

Predictions

Here's your chance to challenge the Editor of the Middlesbrough FC Annual and your best friend in predicting how Boro will do in 2007-08 season and who will win all of football's biggest honours

Boro won the Carling Cup in 2004. But who will win this Season?

		Editor's Prediction	My Prediction	My Best Friend's Prediction

BORO

		Editor's Prediction	My Prediction	My Best Friend's Prediction
1	In what position will Boro finish in the Premier League?	7th		
2	What round will Boro reach in the FA Cup?	Winners!		
3	Who will be Boro's top goalscorer?	Yakubu		
4	Who will win the Boro Supporters Club's player of the year award?	Tuncay		
5	Who will win the Boro Supporters Club's young player of the year award?	Cattermole		

ENGLISH FOOTBALL

		Editor's Prediction	My Prediction	My Best Friend's Prediction
1	Who will be Premier League champions?	Man United		
2	Which three other teams will qualify for the Champions League?	Chelsea Liverpool Tottenham		
3	Which three teams will be relegated from the Premier League?	Wigan Fulham Derby		
4	Who will win the FA Cup?	Boro!		
5	Who will win the Carling Cup?	Liverpool		
6	Who will be the Premier League's top goalscorer?	Ronaldo		

EUROPEAN FOOTBALL

		Editor's Prediction	My Prediction	My Best Friend's Prediction
1	Who will win the Champions League?	Barcelona		
2	Who will win the UEFA Cup?	Tottenham		

INTERNATIONAL FOOTBALL

		Editor's Prediction	My Prediction	My Best Friend's Prediction
1	Which country will win the 2008 European Championships?	France		

Season Review

Was Boro's 2006-07 season mint or minging?

Middlesbrough Football Club 2007/08

Mint Boro finished the season in mid-table to ensure a tenth successive season of Premier League football.

Minging 12th place in the Premier League? Surely that's not good enough.

Mint Boro went goal crazy for two months early in 2007 when Yakubu and Mark Viduka seemed to score in every match.

Minging Goals were hard to come by for most of the season

Mint In his first season as Boro manager, Gareth Southgate led Boro to victory over the champions, Chelsea and great results against Arsenal, Man United and Bolton.

Minging After five cup finals in the past 12 years, Boro could not overcome Man United in the FA Cup Quarter Final

We'll leave you to decide how you feel about a season of stark contrasts. Meanwhile, let's take a trip down memory lane. Rewind to August 2006

August

READING	3	BORO	2
BORO	2	CHELSEA	1
BORO	0	PORTSMOUTH	4

LIKE much of the 2006-07 season, August was a season of contrasting results and performances for Boro. In fact, from the very first game at newly promoted Reading, we saw Boro's best and worst – shooting into a two-goal lead with strikes from Stewart Downing and Yakubu, only to throw it away before half-time and lose the match altogether in the second half. To make matters worse, Julio Arca broke his foot on his debut, joining another new signing, £6 million Robert Huth, on the sidelines.

Gareth Southgate took charge of a Premier League game at the Riverside for the first time four days later and the occasion was made all the more special by the visit of Jose Mourinho's expensively assembled champions, Chelsea. There was much pre-match talk of Chelsea seeking revenge for their humiliating 3-0 Riverside defeat the previous season, but

central defensive convert Emanuel Pogatetz headed a fine equaliser before sub Mark Viduka's last-gasp winner.

Victory over the champions sent Boro into the weekend home clash with bubbling Portsmouth in high spirits but Gareth's greats of a few nights earlier became Southgate's super flops, humbled 4-0 in front a live Sky Sports audience. With eight goals conceded in their first three games, the alarm bells were ringing loud and clear. Next up? A visit to Arsenal, who had struck a magnificent seven on Boro's last visit to London.

September

WE have an official announcement to make – Boro are in crisis! At least that's how it seemed as Boro crashed towards the relegation positions and were victims of a massive cup upset. Even the homecoming of Jonathan Woodgate on a year's loan from Real Madrid could not steady the ship.

Player of the month: Jonathan Woodgate

ARSENAL	1	BORO	1
BOLTON	0	BORO	0
BORO	0	NOTTS COUNTY	1
BORO	0	BLACKBURN	1
SHEFFIELD UNITED	2	BORO	1

Woodgate's arrival certainly helped Boro tighten up at the back but now we were struggling to SCORE! Two impressive draws at sides chasing Europe, Arsenal and Bolton, suggested Boro were heading in the right direction. James Morrison put Boro ahead in their first ever visit to the Emirates Stadium before Arsenal pegged them back.

But it all went pear-shaped again when a much-changed Boro side fell to a disastrous home defeat to League Two visitors Notts County, themselves playing without many of their first choice players.

Days later another desperately poor home display saw Blackburn leave the Riverside with all three points – a result that Gareth Southgate described as "a wake-up call". Boro were better at Bramall Lane in their following game but still lost to a late Phil Jagielka strike as Sheffield United recorded their first victory of the season.

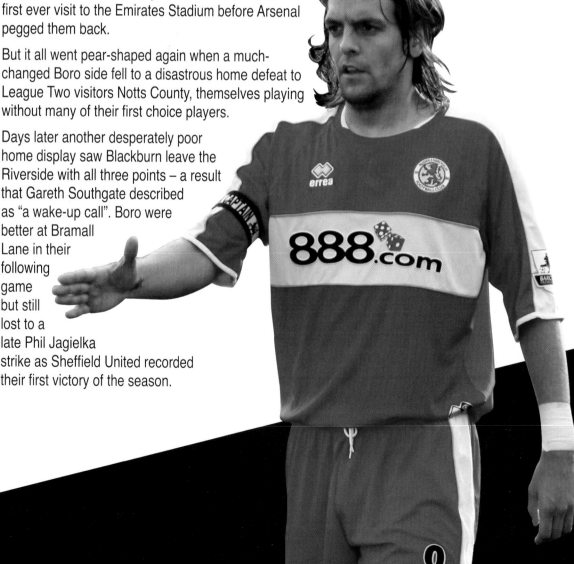

October

THIS was yet another frustrating month for rookie boss Gareth Southgate as he saw his side take two massive steps forward with important wins over high-flying Everton and local rivals Newcastle, only to produce the worst performance of the season so far against Man City at Eastlands.

With Southgate demanding a more attacking approach from his players, Boro turned on the style when Everton visited the Riverside, with twin strikers Viduka and Yakubu securing a fully-deserved victory.

That was followed by a less impressive but even more celebrated win over our north-east neighbours Newcastle, with Yakubu scoring a rare header late in the game to grab all three points and move Boro up to 12th. But the wheels fell off once again with the visit to Manchester City, with a desperately poor display disappointing the travelling army of Boro fans.

Player of the month:		Emanuel Pogatetz	
BORO	2	EVERTON	1
BORO	1	NEWCASTLE UNITED	0
MAN CITY	1	BORO	0

November

WATFORD	2	BORO	0
BORO	1	WEST HAM	0
BORO	0	LIVERPOOL	0
ASTON VILLA	1	BORO	1

IT might not have been the attacking, free-flowing football Gareth Southgate had promised, but Boro finally looked to be heading in the right direction in November. A defence that had conceded eight goals in three games before the arrival of Jonathan Woodgate had now conceded only nine in their last 11 Premier League games. But Woodgate's less-lauded defensive partner Emanuel Pogatetz was perhaps the real hero of the hour.

Boro actually made an awful start to November, with a 2-0 defeat at Vicarage Road handing Watford their first win of the season. If anything it was even worse than the display at Manchester City a few days earlier. But super sub Massimo Maccarone came off the bench to clinch a vital victory over West Ham as Boro recorded a third straight home win.

That was followed by a highly acceptable home draw with Liverpool and then an impressive 1-1 draw at high-flying Aston Villa, whose manager Martin O'Neill had held talks with Boro before Steve Gibson turned to Gareth Southgate. The visit to Villa Park was notable for the

fact that Abel Xavier made his first appearance since completing a year's drugs ban and Malcolm Christie scored his first goal for 21 months.

December

A YEAR that had seen Boro appear in a UEFA Cup final ended with the club just three points above the relegation zone. And with just nine goals scored in their last 12 league games it seemed much would depend on the defensive form for Woodgate, Pogatetz and Schwarzer if they were to avoid dropping into the Championship.

The month began with two frustrating results, the first against league leaders Manchester United, and the second to UEFA Cup hopefuls Tottenham. A controversial penalty awarded when Cristiano Ronaldo was not touched by Mark Schwarzer gave United the lead before Darren Fletcher won the points a minute after James Morrison's deserved equaliser.

Schwarzer was outstanding in a 1-1 home draw with Wigan before more woe at Fulham. The fact that Boro started the day in the bottom three meant the visit to the Riverside of second-bottom Charlton was billed as a crucial "six-pointer". This time Boro turned on

BORO	1	MAN UNITED	2
TOTTENHAM	2	BORO	1
BORO	1	WIGAN	1
FULHAM	2	BORO	1
BORO	2	CHARLTON	0
EVERTON	0	BORO	0
BLACKBURN	2	BORO	1

the style against a hapless Charlton side that sacked Les Reed, their second manager of the season, a few days later. Yakubu and Arca grabbed the crucial goals.

A battling goalless draw against Everton at Goodison Park on Boxing Day brought more reason to be cheerful but the year ended on a low when Blackburn completed a league "double" over Boro at Ewood Park.

January

TWELVE months earlier Boro had been under pressure to sack manager Steve McClaren as Boro fought a desperate relegation battle. One year on and Gareth Southgate ensured no such pressure fell on his shoulders, thanks to a stunning month that saw Boro finish January in the top 10.

Having struggled to score goals all season, Boro were suddenly transformed into the nation's most free-scoring side, scoring 18 goals in their first six games of the month as strikers Mark Viduka and Yakubu proved unstoppable.

Viduka scored six goals, starting with two as Boro let in the New Year in style with an excellent 3-1 win over their fellow relegation-strugglers Sheffield United. That was followed with a first away win of the season, another three-goal show at Charlton, with Arca, Yakubu and Cattermole all on target after former Riverside hero Jimmy Floyd Hasselbaink had fired the home side ahead.

Suddenly Boro's confidence was bubbling but no one could have predicted the five-star performance against Champions League

Player of the month: Mark Viduka			
BORO	3	SHEFFIELD UNITED	1
HULL CITY	1	BORO	1
CHARLTON	1	BORO	3
BORO	4	HULL CITY	3
BORO	5	BOLTON	1
BRISTOL	2	BORO	2
PORTSMOUTH	0	BORO	0

hopefuls Bolton Wanderers. Boro were three up inside 23 minutes and led 4-1 at half-time in a game that saw England winger Stewart Downing in magical form, scoring one and setting up three.

Meanwhile, progress was slow in the FA Cup, with Hull City beaten in a replay in a seven-goal thriller at the Riverside before League Two side Bristol City forced a replay after being two goals behind at Ashton Gate.

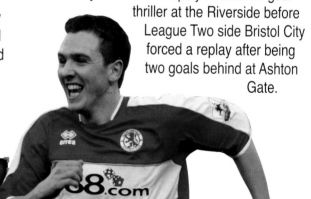

February

THE relegation fears of the turn of the year now seemed long forgotten as Boro built on their wonderful January form with another highly positive four weeks in February, reaching the last eight of the FA Cup and continuing their Premier League progress.

With Julio Arca now controlling games from his new position as the club's creative midfielder, Boro were looking a different side from the one that had relied so much on their defensive skills earlier in the season. And in Yakubu and Mark Viduka, each with nine goals in 2007, Boro now had the Premier League's two most prolific strikers.

Yakubu's penalty ensured a 1-1 league draw with Arsenal as Boro stretched their unbeaten run to eight games. A first defeat of the 2007 finally came against Chelsea, though the 3-0 scoreline flattered the champions. Then came another excellent result as Boro exacted revenge for their opening day defeat at Reading, as Steve Coppell's high-fliers were beaten 2-1 at the Riverside with yet more goals from

Player of the month: Julio Arca			
BORO	1	ARSENAL	1
CHELSEA	3	BORO	0
BORO	2	BRISTOL CITY	2
WEST BROM	2	BORO	2
BORO	2	READING	1
BORO	1	WEST BROM	1

Viduka and Yakubu.

Progress in the FA Cup continued – though it was touch and go at times. Twice Boro had to rely on their penalty shoot-out skills after failing to beat lower division opposition in highly entertaining Riverside replays, eventually winning both shoot-outs 5-4.

March

THIS was the month when Boro's wheels fell off again! It all started to go wrong as we prepared for an FA Cup quarter-final replay with Manchester United, full of belief that we could win at Old Trafford on the back of a run that had seen us lose just once in 15 games since the turn of the year.

Player of the month: Jonathan Woodgate			
NEWCASTLE UNITED	0	BORO	0
BORO	2	MAN UNITED	2
BORO	0	MAN CITY	2
MAN UNITED	1	BORO	0
WEST HAM	2	BORO	0

A battling, if forgettable, goalless derby draw at Newcastle was followed by a mega quarter-final clash with Man U at the Riverside. Boro looked destined for the semi-final after goals from Lee Cattermole and George Boateng either side of half-time fired us in front after Wayne Rooney had opened the scoring for United. But Ronaldo scored from the spot after a penalty was awarded against Boateng for using his hands – and now Boro faced a trip to Old Trafford.

United dominated much of the replay but Mark Schwarzer was in outstanding form. Eventually, only another controversial penalty decision – with Ronaldo again the scorer – took United through to a semi-final against Watford.

The drama of the cup resulted in Boro taking their eyes off the ball in terms of Premier League points. Boro got what they deserved in a 2-0 home defeat to Manchester City days before the United replay and then seemed to suffer a cup hangover when relegation-threatened West Ham won their first home game for three months.

April

TWELVE months earlier Boro had been fighting for cup glory on two fronts, appearing in the semi-finals of both the FA and UEFA Cups. Now they had only Premier League points to battle for – and they were finding them hard to come by.

A 4-1 demolition of rock-bottom Watford was a return to top form, with two-goal Mark Viduka and teenage winger Adam Johnson the stars of the show. But seven days later came a poor 3-1 home defeat to Aston Villa, before a visit to Anfield brought a fifth defeat in six games.

Perhaps the highlight of the month was a 1-1 draw at Old Trafford, with Viduka scoring an outstanding header from Downing's cross to equalise – and Dong Gook Lee denied a definite penalty in the dying seconds.

But the month ended with another defeat, leaving relegation a possible, if unlikely, outcome with just two games remaining.

Player of the month: Fabio Rochemback				
BORO	4	WATFORD	1
BORO	1	ASTON VILLA	3
LIVERPOOL	2	BORO	0
MAN UNITED	1	BORO	1
BORO	2	TOTTENHAM	3

May

A SEASON of highs and lows ended on a positive note and a 12th place finish as back-to-back victories – Boro's first since January – ensured Gareth Southgate finished well clear of the bottom three in a difficult first season as manager.

That man Mark Viduka was again on target to give Boro a vital victory at Wigan in the final away match. Paul Jewell's side were desperate for the points but failed to threaten a Boro side that could still have gone down if results had gone against them.

With relegation no longer a possibility, bubbling Boro played some champagne football in their final match of the season. Boro scored three but might easily have had six or seven as they sent the fans home happy for the summer. Top scorer Mark Viduka signed off in style with two goals, taking his tally for the season to 19 – and 42 in just 80 starts in a Boro shirt. Riverside fans cheered him from the pitch but hoped that, with his contract running out, it would not be his last

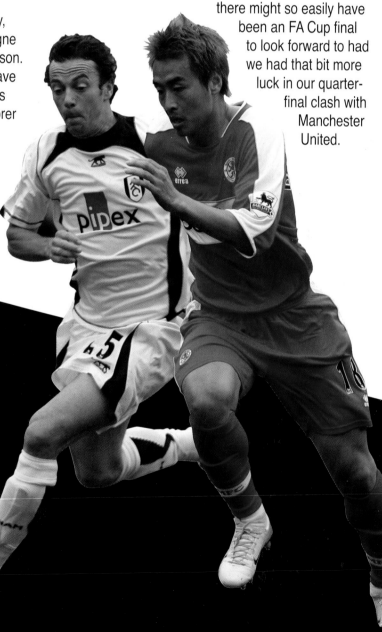

game for the club. Sadly, he would join Newcastle United over the summer.

For Gareth Southgate, there was every reason to feel satisfied. A mid-table finish had been achieved, Boro were the north-east's top team, having finished above Newcastle United, and there might so easily have been an FA Cup final to look forward to had we had that bit more luck in our quarter-final clash with Manchester United.

Highlights of the courses include:

- Learn new skills from qualified coaches!
- Take part in shoot-out competitions to win top prizes!
- Have a great time instead of being bored at home!

Play Like The Stars

For further information about Boro's mega coaching courses, call

01642 282128

or visit Middlesbrough Football Club in the Community's own website

mfcic.co.uk.

If you live on Teesside, then there's never any need to be bored during the school holidays - because Boro's coaching courses are sure to be available somewhere close.

Boro's superb Football in the Community courses are perfect for all young Boro fans, whether they are boys or girls.

The Boro courses are designed for all abilities aged from 3-14, so there's sure to be a course just right for you.

The courses include specialist coaching for goalkeepers, 'micro soccer' for three to five-year-olds, 'mini soccer' for five to seven-year-olds, girls-only sessions and coaching for players with disabilities.

What's more, there's even the chance you could meet a Boro star on one of the courses. Riverside heroes like Stewart Downing, Mark Schwarzer, Lee Cattermole and Emanuel Pogatetz have all been along to recent coaching sessions to talk to fans, sign autographs and hand out prizes.

The courses take place at bases in Eston, Stockton, Billingham, Yarm, Redcar, Guisborough, Ingleby Barwick, Stokesley, Thirsk, Richmond, Bedale, Boroughbridge and Northallerton.

Where in the world?

Have a look at our world map to see which countries Boro stars were born in

Emanuel Pogatetz
Steinbock, Austria

Tuncay Sanli
Sakarya, Turkey

George Boateng
Accra, Ghana

Stewart Downing
Middlesbrough, United Kingdom

Jonathan Woodgate
Middlesbrough, United Kingdom

Fabio Rochemback
Soledade, Brazil

Julio Arca
Capital Federal, Argentina

Yakubu
Benin, Nigeria

Jeremie Aliadiere
Rambouillet, France

Robert Huth
Berlin, Germany

Brad Jones
Armadale, Australia

Mark Schwarzer
Sydney, Australia

Dong Gook Lee
South Korea

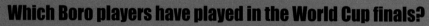

Ask us a Question

Your questions answered on all things Boro!

Which Boro players have played in the World Cup finals?

There have been only 10 Boro players who have appeared for their country in the finals of a World Cup tournament – and only four of them played for England!

The first Boro star to play at the World Cup was Wilf Mannion, a forward that many fans who saw him play insist was Boro's greatest player ever. Mannion played twice for England in the 1950 World Cup in Brazil.

Twelve years later, in 1962, another forward Alan Peacock also played twice for England against Argentina and Bulgaria. It was another 20 years before Northern Ireland goalkeeper Jim Platt became the third Boro World Cup star.

Over the past 10 years, however, seven more Boro heroes have played in the World Cup. Paul Merson was part of the England squad at the 1998 finals, when striker Hamilton Ricard also played for Colombia.

At the 2002 tournament, Boro were represented by Alen Boksic of Croatia and Joseph-Desire Job of Cameroon. Then, at the last World Cup in 2006, Stewart Downing played for England, while Australia's team included Boro stars Mark Schwarzer and Mark Viduka.

Have any Boro players published books?

It's surprising just how many current or former Boro players have published books. Goalkeeper Mark Schwarzer wrote a fictional children's story in 2007, 10 years after telling the story of Boro's 1997-98 promotion season in Mark My Words.

Two years before that, another Boro shot-stopper, Alan Miller, had also told the story of a season in a book called A Miller's Tale, while former striker John Hendrie's autobiography, Don't Call Me Happy, was a big seller.

Perhaps the most successful life story by a former Boro player was 'Extra Time' by 1970s star Willie Maddren, with sales of the book raising £40,000 for research into Motor Neurone Disease.

But the former Boro player to have brought out most books must surely be Bernie Slaven. One of the club's all-time top goalscorers, Bernie has published two autobiographies of his life, Strikingly Different and Legend? Along with his co-commentator Alastair Brownlee, he also wrote The Road to Eindhoven and joined up with Eric

Gates and Malcolm Macdonald for another book called The Three Legends.

And we mustn't forget Boro manager Gareth Southgate, who wrote a book called Woody and Nord with his best friend, Andy Woodman, about how they remained friends throughout their two very different football careers.

I read in the newspaper that all footballers drive Ferraris and Bentleys? Is that really what the Boro players drive?

That's not quite true, though Fabio Rochemback does drive a red Ferrari. All the players drive great cars but they are not all as flashy as a Ferrari!

For instance, Andrew Taylor's car is an Audi RS4, Jonathan Woodgate drives a Mercedes, as does Robert Huth because the German international only drives cars from the country of his birth!

Yakubu drives a fantastic Porsche Cayenne, but the most surprising car driven by a Boro star has to be Emanuel Pogatetz's Mini, complete with a Union Jack on its roof!

28

Yakubu has scored lots of penalties for Boro. Has anyone scored more Boro penalties?

It's true, Yakubu has proved himself to be a fantastic penalty-taker for Boro. The Nigerian is always very cool from the spot, usually placing the ball gently to either side of the goalkeeper and never hitting it hard!

In his first two seasons with Boro, he scored 11 penalties – but that still meant six other players had scored more spot-kicks than Yakubu.

1960s midfielder Arthur Kaye scored 14 penalties for Boro, while pre-war striker George Elliott scored 20 of his total of over 200 goals from the penalty spot. Ahead of Elliott is Jamaican forward Lindy Delapenha with 22 penalties during the 1950s.

During the 1950s and 1960s, Welsh midfielder Bill Harris rarely missed a penalty and scored 25 in all. But easily the club's all-time greatest penalty-taker was striker John Hickton, who scored an incredible 36 penalties during the 1960s and 1970s. 'Big John' was famed for taking very long runs before whacking the ball with all his might, usually giving the opposition 'keeper no chance!

Chelsea's squad cost over £200 million, but how much did Boro's cost?

Boro's squad was definitely a bargain compared to Chelsea's! One of the most expensive players of the Boro squad that started the 2007-08 season was last summer's big signing from Real Madrid, Jonathan Woodgate, who cost £7 million.

But other current Boro players that cost big fees are Yakubu (£7.5 million), Robert Huth (£6 million), George Boateng (£5 million), Jeremie Aliadiere (£2 million), Emanuel Pogatetz (£1.8 million), Julio Arca (£1.75 million), Chris Riggott (£1.5 million) and Mark Schwarzer (£1.25 million).

But remember other stars like Stewart Downing, Lee Cattermole, Andrew Taylor, Andrew Davies, Brad Jones and Ross Turnbull cost nothing because they came from Boro's youth team, while there was no fee for Tuncay Sanli or Dong Gook Lee. The total cost of the Boro squad was £34.6 million.

10 Things You Didn't Know About The Boro Players!

1 Defender Tony McMahon, who made his first team debut against Manchester United at Old Trafford, was first spotted by Boro after **HIS MUM** wrote to the club asking to give "our Anthony" a trial!

2 Andrew Taylor must have **NIGHTMARES** about his first team debut for Boro, as it came in a 7-0 defeat at Arsenal in January 2006!

3 Emanuel Pogatetz has played football for seven teams in **FIVE** different countries. He started out in his home country of Austria before moving to Germany, Switzerland and Russia before moving to England with Boro!

4 Tuncay Sanli (bottom left) became the first Turkish player **EVER** to score a hat-trick in the Champions League when he scored all three goals in Fenerbahce's 3-0 win over Manchester United in 2004!

5 Lee Cattermole became the **YOUNGEST EVER** Boro captain when he was given the captain's armband at Fulham for the final league game of the 2005-06 season. Lee was just six weeks past his 18th birthday!

6 The **ONLY** Boro player ever to play more games for England than Stewart Downing is the great Wilf Mannion, who appeared for his country 26 times during the 1940s and 1950s!

7 Julio Arca was a member of the Argentina squad that **WON** the World Youth Championships in 2001!

8 Yakubu once scored four goals **AGAINST** Boro in our 5-1 defeat at Portsmouth on the last day of the 2003-04 season!

9 Adam Johnson (above) and David Wheater made their Boro debuts as subs in the last 16 of the **UEFA Cup** against Sporting Lisbon!

10 Jonathan Woodgate joined Boro for £7 million in the summer of 2007 – 11 years after leaving the club's youth team for Leeds for **ABSOLUTELY NOTHING**!

Spot the
difference

Look closely at the pictures below. Can you find all six differences?

Answers on page 61

Have you ever met a Boro player? If not, you must go around with your eyes closed because your Riverside heroes are always out and about in the local community

Community Champions!

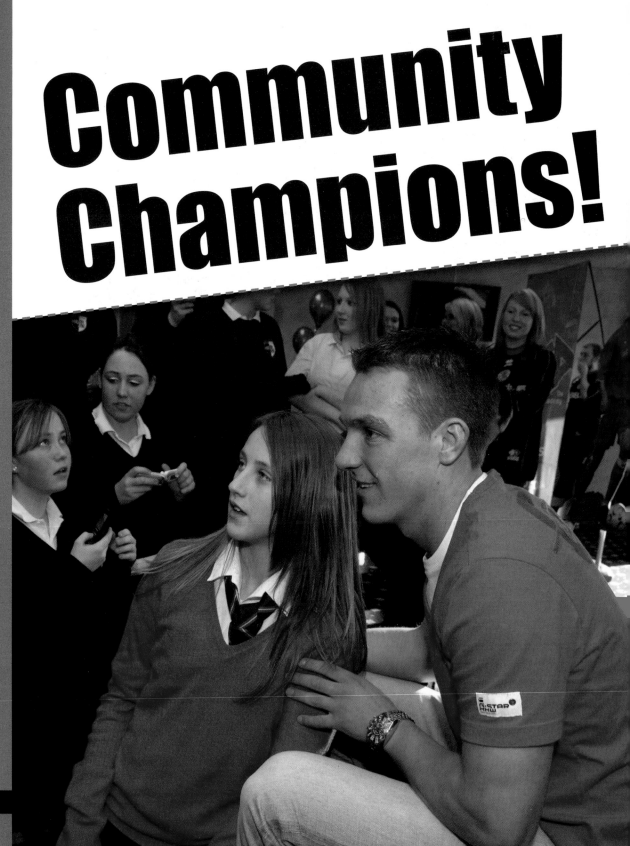

❝ …they know what it will mean to young fans to get a chance to meet their heroes ❞

Boro players aren't just stars on the pitch. They are also superstars off it. Every year Middlesbrough spend more time in the local community, meeting fans and helping charities than almost any other club.

Manager Gareth Southgate and his players spend many hours meeting young Boro fans through the club's wide range of education and fitness projects.

In fact, last season Boro stars made more than 300 appearances in the local community, including:

- Christmas visits to see poorly children in hospital.
- Talks to boys and girls about why racism is wrong.
- Question-and-answer sessions with young fans about the dangers of smoking – and why it's important to have a healthy diet.
- Helping charities and good causes.
- Coaching sessions with Boro fans to show them why exercise is so great.

Stars like Jonathan Woodgate, Stewart Downing, Lee Cattermole, Andrew Taylor, Julio Arca and Emanuel Pogatetz all give up their own spare time to go and meet young fans like you because they know what it will mean to young fans to get a chance to meet their heroes.

So next time you're out and about on Teesside, make sure you keep your eyes open – because there might just be a Boro player out and about for you to meet!

Player Profiles

BRAD JONES

Position: Goalkeeper

Previous clubs: Shelbourne (loan), Stockport (loan), Rotherham (loan), Blackpool (loan), Sheffield Wednesday (loan)

International honours: Australia full caps

Date of birth: March 19th 1982

BEING a deputy can be a frustrating job – especially when you are second choice to the same man for club and country! That is the reality for goalkeeper Brad Jones, who is able cover for Mark Schwarzer for both Boro and Australia.

Jones made his long-awaited international debut for his country against Uruguay during the summer of 2007, having been in the shadow of his good friend Schwarzer for several years.

Although an Australian, Jones is actually a product of Boro's Academy. He gained first team experience with several clubs before making the breakthrough at Boro and enjoyed a long loan spell with Sheffield Wednesday last season.

MARK SCHWARZER

Position: Goalkeeper

Previous clubs: Marconi Stallions, Dinamo Dresden, Kaiserslautern, Bradford City.

International honours: Australia full caps

Date of birth: October 6th 1982

TALENTED goalkeeper Mark Schwarzer has made more Premier League appearances for Boro than anyone else – and has played more games at the Riverside Stadium than any other player.

Rated one of the best 'keepers in the Premier League over the last 10 years, Schwarzer has been with Boro longer than any other member of the current squad.

Former Boro manager Bryan Robson signed the Aussie from Bradford City for £1.25 million in January 1997 after Schwarzer had failed to win a regular place in Germany with Dinamo Dresden and Kaiserslautern.

He was a losing finalist with Boro in the 1997 and 1998 League Cup finals before helping bring the Carling Cup to Teesside in 2004 when Bolton were beaten in the final at the Millennium Stadium.

Schwarzer, who returned to Germany to play for Australia in the 2006 World Cup finals shortly after helping Boro reach the UEFA Cup final, has won more international caps with Boro than any other player in the club's long history.

ANDREW DAVIES

Position: Right-back/Central defender

Previous clubs: Derby (loan)

International honours: England Under-21

Date of birth: December 17th 1984

DAVIES enjoyed his best ever season as a Boro player in 2006-07 when he fought off challenges from Abel Xavier, Stuart Parnaby and Tony McMahon to be the club's regular choice at right-back.

Although he admits to preferring a central defensive role, the Stockton lad is proud to represent his local team and has spurned interest from other clubs to stay on and challenge for Gareth Southgate's side.

Yet another product of Boro's fine Academy, Davies captained Boro to the 2003 FA Youth Cup final, where they lost narrowly to Manchester United. By then, he had already made his first team debut.

ANDREW TAYLOR

Position: Left back

Previous clubs: Bradford City (loan)

International honours: England Under-21

Date of birth: August 1st 1986

A LOAN spell in League One with Bradford City proved to be the best thing that could have happened to Andrew Taylor. On his return to the Riverside, he enjoyed a fantastic second half to the 2005-06 season, appearing in the UEFA and FA Cup semi-finals while still a teenager.

He then made the left-back spot his own when Gareth Southgate succeeded Steve McClaren as Boro manager, rarely missing a game throughout 2006-07.

Yet another product of the club's Academy, Hartlepool-born Taylor played in midfield when he was part of the Boro side that won the FA Youth Cup in 2004. His progress was delayed when injury forced him to miss most of the 2004-05 season but he was a great success on loan to Bradford, earning an England Under-21 call-up.

EMANUEL POGATETZ

Position: Central defender

Previous clubs: Sturm Graz, Karnten, Bayer Leverkusen, Aurau (loan), Grazer AK (loan), Spartak Moscow (loan)

International honours: Austria full caps

Date of birth: January 16th 1983

AUSTRIAN defender Emanuel Pogatetz was once nicknamed 'Mad Dog' by Boro fans because of his aggressive tackling and bad temper! But by the end of the 2006-07 season he was the fans' 'Top Dog' instead, as he was named the Supporters Club Player of the Year.

Pogatetz was signed for a £1.8 million fee from German side Bayer Leverkusen, having caught Boro's attention when facing the club in UEFA Cup action while on loan to Austrian side, Grazer AK.

Originally signed as a left-back, he was switched to central defence when Robert Huth and Chris Riggott were injured, performing so well that neither could win back their place.

Before moving to England, Pogatetz had already played in Austria, Germany, Switzerland and Russia. He hopes to play for Austria when his country hosts the 2008 European Championships.

MATTHEW BATES

Position: Central defender

Previous clubs: Darlington (loan), Ipswich Town (loan)

International honours: England youth

Date of birth: December 10th 1986

SERIOUS injury meant Middlesbrough-born Bates struggled to follow up what had been a memorable 2005-06 campaign last season.

Another former member of Boro's 2004 FA Youth Cup winners, Bates has often impressed when given his chance at Boro, mainly at centre-back but also filling in as an emergency right-back.

His proudest moment came in Romania when he produced a superb central defensive performance as Boro took a big step towards the UEFA Cup final with a battling display against Steaua Bucharest.

However, injury and the form of Jonathan Woodgate and Emanuel Pogatetz meant he rarely got a look in last season when he even suffered injury problems during a loan spell with Ipswich Town.

CHRIS RIGGOTT

Position: **Centre-back**
Previous clubs: **Derby**
International honours: **England Under-21**
Date of birth: **February 17th 1980**

CLASSY Chris Riggott was looking to bounce back to his best in 2007-08 after suffering a year of injury problems last season when Jonathan Woodgate and Emanuel Pogatetz established themselves as Boro's first choice central defenders.

Riggott had previously been one of Boro's first choice centre-backs alongside his present day manager Gareth Southgate, producing a string of fine performances during the runs to the UEFA Cup final and FA Cup semi-final in 2006, culminating in his selection as the Boro players' player of the year.

Riggott joined Boro from hometown club Derby in January 2003 as part of a £3 million deal that also saw Malcolm Christie make the move to the Riverside.

JONATHAN WOODGATE

Position: **Central defender**
Previous clubs: **Leeds United, Newcastle United, Real Madrid**
International honours: **England full caps**
Date of birth: **January 22nd 1980**

BORO pulled off a huge coup that shocked many of the game's so-called experts when Jonathan Woodgate agreed a permanent £7 million transfer from Spanish giant Real Madrid in April 2007.

The Nunthorpe-born defender had returned home to Teesside initially on a year's loan, with many people suggesting Boro were taking a huge risk on a player whose obvious talent had been clouded by injuries in the past.

But Woodgate's sensational form at the heart of Boro's defence not only earned him the Player of the Year award but an England recall against Spain.

Having been on Boro's books as a youngster, Woodgate made his name with Leeds United before spells with Newcastle United and Real Madrid.

GAIZKA MENDIETA

Position: Midfielder
Previous clubs: Castellon, Valencia, Lazio, Barcelona
International honours: Spain full caps
Date of birth: March 27th 1974

BORO snapped up Mendieta on a free transfer 'bargain' during the summer of 2003, just two years after the Spain international had joined Italian side Lazio from Valencia for £28.9 million.

Whilst with the Spanish side, Mendieta earned a reputation as Europe's finest midfielder, inspiring them to successive Champions League finals before his big-money move to Rome.

He has enjoyed mixed fortunes in the red and white of Boro, playing his part in bringing the Carling Cup to the Riverside in 2004 but also suffering from injury and then finding himself out of favour since Gareth Southgate became manager.

ROBERT HUTH

Position: Central defender
Previous club: Chelsea
International honours: Germany full caps
Date of birth: August 18 1984

IT was fair to say that Boro fans saw only the tip of the iceberg in terms of Robert Huth's undoubted talents during his first season at the Riverside.

Signed for £6 million from then champions Chelsea aged just 22, Huth was already a regular for the German international team when Gareth Southgate brought him to Teesside in the summer of 2006.

But injuries meant he sat out too much of his first year with Boro, though he showed Riverside regulars what they were missing with some fine performances in central defence whenever he was fit.

Huth will be looking to put real pressure on Jonathan Woodgate and Emanuel Pogatetz for a regular starting place in the Boro defence in 2007-08.

FABIO ROCHEMBACK

Position: Midfielder
Previous clubs: Internacional, Barcelona, Sporting Lisbon (loan)
International honours: Brazil full caps
Date of birth: December 10th 1981

IS Fabio Rochemback a good luck charm or bad omen? That's what fans should wonder given his amazing record in the UEFA Cup. While on loan to Sporting Lisbon he help the Portuguese side reach the 2005 UEFA Cup final, but had to be content with a losers' medal. Just 12 months later, he was back in the same final, this time with Boro – and was again on the losing side.

It was the Brazilian midfielder's performances in helping Sporting knock Boro out of the UEFA Cup that convinced former Riverside boss Steve McClaren to bring him to England.

He initially struggled to find his best form before becoming a key player for the club. He again lost his place under Gareth Southgate's management but bounced back with some fine performances late in the 2006-07 season and says he wants to see out his five-year Boro contract.

The midfield play-maker made his name in Brazil with Internacional and won full caps for his country after a big-money move to Spanish giants Barcelona.

STEWART DOWNING

Position: Left winger
Previous club: Sunderland (loan)
International honours: England full caps
Date of birth: July 22nd 1984

ONLY Boro legend Wilf Mannion has won more England caps as a Middlesbrough player than young winger Stewart Downing, who has been a regular in the national squad under Sven Goran Eriksson and Steve McClaren.

The speedy left-footer, born in Middlesbrough's Pallister Park estate, has been Boro's main creative force for the last four seasons, ever since proving himself during a loan spell to our north-east rivals Sunderland.

He has been linked with a £10 million move to Tottenham in the past but has made it clear that he loves nothing better than playing for his hometown club.

DAVID WHEATER

Position: Defender
Previous clubs: Darlington (loan)
International honours: England Youth
Date of birth: February 14th 1987

Young defender David Wheater finished the 2006-07 season on a huge high with his first ever goal on the final day of the campaign - and started 2007-08 where he left off by making the team for the opening day. No doubt he will be hoping this will be his big breakthrough season despite competition from so many experienced central defenders.

The centre-back is a product of Boro's much-lauded Academy, having been a part of the team that won the 2004 FA Youth Cup. He played in the Youth Cup final success against Aston Villa just 12 months after losing the 2003 final to Manchester United. His partnership with Matthew Bates at youth and reserve levels continued into the first team as they formed Boro's central defence against Fulham on the final day of the 2005-06 season.

Wheater spent much of last season gaining valuable League experience at the heart of Darlington's defence but returned to the Riverside in time to play against Fulham on the final day of the campaign. He played his part in the 3-1 victory, scoring a fine header.

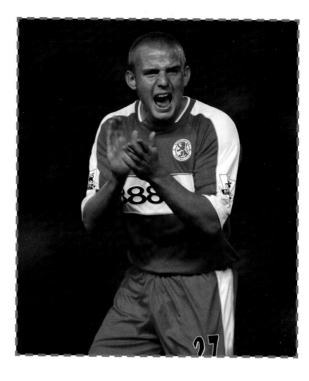

LEE CATTERMOLE

Position: Central midfielder
Previous clubs: None
International honours: England youth
Date of birth: March 21st 1988

STOCKTON-born midfielder Lee Cattermole made a dramatic entry to the Riverside first team during the latter part of the 2005-06 season, having made his Premier League debut at Newcastle United on New Year's Day.

His combative and classy displays made it look like Cattermole had been playing in the Boro midfield for years, but he had in fact only established a regular place in the club's reserve side earlier the same season.

Cattermole became the club's youngest ever captain, aged just 18, on the final day of the 2005-06 Premier League when Boro played a side almost entirely made up of former Academy players.

Although frequently played out of his favoured central midfield role during 2006-07, often as a stand-in right winger, Cattermole continued to impress.

JULIO ARCA

Position: **Central midfield/left-back**
Previous clubs: **Argentinos Juniors, Sunderland**
International honours: **Argentina Youth**
Date of birth: **May 31st 1981**

THE midfield performances of Julio Arca were one of Boro's surprise packages last season. The surprise was not so much the Argentinian's form as the fact that he proved such a revelation in a central midfield role.

Gareth Southgate had signed Arca to replace Franck Queudrue as the club's regular left-back but a broken foot on the opening day of the season gave Andrew Taylor a chance to stake his claim for the position – and Arca was eventually asked to slot in to a creative midfield role.

Despite never having previously played there, he adapted to the change of position so well that he became an automatic choice. His range of passing and silky skills were a delight to watch, resulting in Southgate recommending him for the Argentina national side.

Arca had made his name with Boro's north-east rivals Sunderland, scoring a fine free-kick in their shock 2-0 win at the Riverside in 2005-06.

ADAM JOHNSON

Position: **Left winger**
Previous clubs: **Leeds United (loan)**
International honours: **England youth**
Date of birth: **July 14 1987**

A BRIGHT future is predicted for England youth winger Johnson, whose tricky skills and crossing ability have already made him a big favourite with Riverside regulars.

A sub in the club's 2004 FA Youth Cup victory, he continued his progress to follow fellow left winger Stewart Downing into the first team, making his first team debut as a sub against Sporting Lisbon in the 2005 UEFA Cup.

He continue to sparkle whenever given an opportunity last season, though Downing's former on the left wing meant he often had to try his luck on the right-hand side of Boro's midfield.

GEORGE BOATENG

Position: **Central midfielder**
Previous clubs: **Excelsior, Feyenoord, Coventry, Aston Villa**
International honours: **Holland full caps**
Date of birth: **September 5th 1975**

WHEN Boro captain Gareth Southgate succeeded Steve McClaren as Middlesbrough manager in the summer of 2006 one of his first decisions was to make George Boateng the club's new skipper.

A hard-working and tough-tackling midfielder, Boateng has become hugely popular with Riverside regulars since joining Boro from Coventry City for £5 million in 2002.

His fine form with the Teesside club, including an appearance in the Carling Cup final victory over Bolton in 2004, earned him a recall to the Holland squad, though he was bitterly disappointed to be left out of their final 23 for the 2006 World Cup finals.

Boateng came to England after playing European football for top Dutch side Feyenoord and impressed at both Coventry and Aston Villa, where his team-mates included Gareth Southgate.

JASON EUELL

Position: **Midfielder**
Previous clubs: **Wimbledon, Charlton Athletic**
International honours: **Jamaica full caps**
Date of birth: **February 6th 1977**

BORO boss Gareth Southgate handed Jason Euell an opportunity to re-launch his career when he agreed a nominal transfer fee with Charlton Athletic for the Lambeth-born Jamaica international in the summer of 2006.

Euell had made his name in the Premier League with Wimbledon, scoring 19 league goals in 2000-01, form that resulted in Charlton paying £4.75m for his services. He justified the outlay by top-scoring for the Addicks for the next three seasons before falling out of favour with their then manager Alan Curbishley.

Euell was mainly used in midfield during his first season with Boro and struggled to make an impact after an initial good run in the first team.

DONG GOOK LEE

Position: Striker

Previous clubs: Pohang Steelers, Werder Bremen (loan), Gwangju Sangmu

International honours: South Korea full caps

Date of birth: April 29th 1979

AIYEGBENI YAKUBU

Position: Striker

Previous clubs: Hapoel Kfar-Saba, Maccabi Haifa, Portsmouth

International honours: Nigeria full caps

Date of birth: November 22nd 1984

ONLY Thierry Henry has scored more Premier League goals than Yakubu over the last four years. That's the form that convinced Boro to part with a £7.5 million fee to bring the Nigerian striker from Portsmouth during the summer of 2005.

Although born in Africa, Yakubu made his name in Israel, famously scoring for Maccabi Haifa against Manchester United in the Champions League. Soon after, he was on his way to the Premiership with Portsmouth.

'The Yak' was a prolific goalscorer with Pompey and scored four goals in a 5-1 win over Boro on the final day of the 2003-04 season. Boro tried to sign Yakubu that summer but eventually got their man 12 months later. He was the club's 19-goal top scorer in his first season on Teesside and followed that with another 16 last year.

A SUPERSTAR back home in South Korea, Dong Gook Lee was an unknown quantity in England when Gareth Southgate gave him an 18-month Boro contract in January 2007.

The striker had impressed the Boro manager during a trial at Rockliffe Park and he was handed several opportunities in the first team during the latter part of the 2006-07 campaign.

Lee, who had a previous short spell in Europe with top German side Werder Bremen in 2000-01, has won over 60 caps for South Korea, where he is known as "The Lion King". Boro fans will hope that he roars into his best form in 2007-08.

NEW SIGNING

TUNCAY SANLI

Position: Striker/Midfielder
Previous clubs: Sakaryaspor, Fenerbahce
International honours: Turkey full caps
Date of birth: January 16th 1982

Fenerbahce fans were shocked when their hero left the Turkish champions to join Boro in June 2007. Nicknamed "Cesur Yurek" or "Brave Heart", Tuncay's ability to run with the ball and willingness to work hard for the team had made him one of Turkey's star players, so Boro pulled off a major coup to sign him on a free transfer at the end of his Fenerbahce contract.

Tuncay's goals and skills had inspired his side to three Turkish championships in just four seasons and he had become the club's all-time top scorer in European competitions, but the player was desperate for a chance to prove himself in the English Premier League so snapped at the chance to join Boro.

A regular goalscorer for Turkey in more than 40 appearances for his country, he once scored a Champions League hat-trick in a 3-0 victory over Manchester United. He also scored three goals for Turkey against Switzerland in a 2006 World Cup play-off qualifier – but the 4-2 victory was not enough, as the Swiss had won the first leg 2-0 and went to the World Cup on the away goals rule.

Although not a big name in England before his move to Teesside, Tuncay was arguably the biggest star of Turkish football, resulting in hundreds of Fenerbahce fans emailing Boro to say they would switch their loyalty to Middlesbrough. In fact, during June 2007, when Tuncay joined Boro, more than half of the visitors to Boro's official website lived in Turkey!

> " I promise Boro fans I will play with my heart and always give my best. "

NEW SIGNING

JEREMIE ALIADIERE

Position: Striker
Previous clubs: Arsenal, Celtic (loan), West Ham (loan), Wolves (loan)
International honours: France U-21 caps
Date of birth: March 30th 1983

Aliadiere replaced Thierry Henry when he made his first team debut for Arsenal in 2002 – but he never came close to fulfilling his dream of replacing the Gunners legend in the hearts of their fans. It was ironic that Henry left Arsenal for Barcelona just two weeks after Aliadiere made the move to Boro, as the speedy striker had lived in the shadow of his fellow Frenchman for so long.

But Gareth Southgate hoped that Aliadiere's frustration at never being given a long first team run at Arsenal would benefit Boro. The Riverside manager paid £2 million for the player in the belief that he would show Arsenal fans what they had missed if he was given the chance to show off his skills on a regular basis.

A product of the famous Clairefontain Academy in France, Aliadiere joined Arsenal when he was just 16 and helped them win the FA Youth Cup in 2001 when his junior team-mates included Jermaine Pennant, Moritz Volz and Steve Sidwell, who have also gone on to big things with clubs other than Arsenal.

Although recognised for his blistering pace and outstanding skill, Aliadiere failed to win a regular Premier League place at Arsenal, though he played a big role in helping the club reach the 2007 Carling Cup final, starring in a 6-3 quarter-final victory at Liverpool and scoring in the semi-final win over Tottenham.

" Joining Middlesbrough is my chance to play regular football after a frustrating time at Arsenal. "

NEW SIGNING

> " Boro are my first priority but I would love to win more England caps too. "

LUKE YOUNG

Position: Right-back
Previous clubs: Tottenham, Charlton Athletic
International honours: England Full caps
Date of birth: July 19th 1979

Luke Young became Gareth Southgate's fourth 2007 summer capture when he made a £2.5 million switch from relegated Charlton Athletic. The right-back arrived at the Riverside determined to win back his place in the England squad, having already won seven full caps.

Young was expected to make the right-back slot his own despite competition from the likes of Andrew Davies and Tony McMahon. No player fully established themselves in the position in 2006-07 with the now departed Abel Xavier and Stuart Parnaby also playing games there.

The player began his career with Tottenham in 1998 but he made a £4 million move to Charlton in the summer of 2001, spending six seasons as the Robins' regular right-back before his switch to the Riverside. He was hopeful that by staying in the Premier League with Boro he could force his way back into the England team after a two-year absence.

After signing for Boro, Young said: "I'm absolutely delighted with this move. Charlton were very understanding when I told them that I wanted to move to ensure I was playing in the Premier League. I loved my time there but this is a great opportunity for me and I want to ensure I make the best of it.

"I feel that playing well for a club like Boro can help me get noticed by the national team. Boro are my first priority but I would love to win more England caps too. I feel my best years are ahead of me and the likes of Gareth Southgate and Colin Cooper - both former England defenders - can help me improve my game."

Lee Cattermole

Crossword Quiz

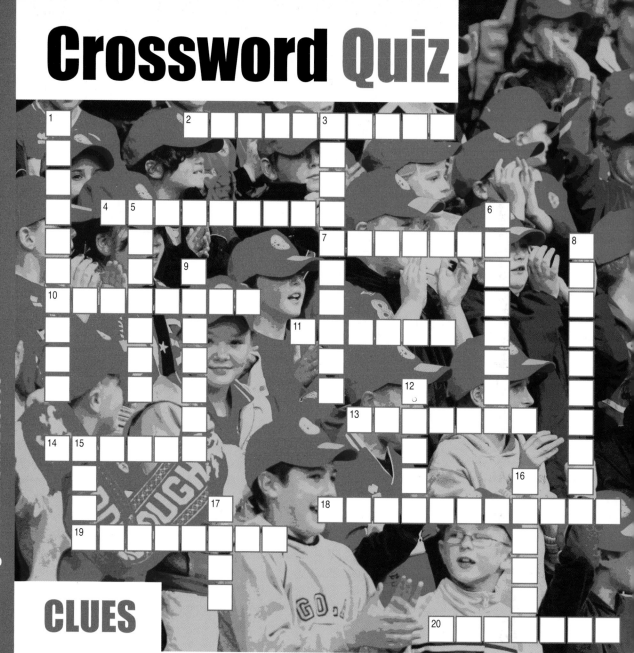

CLUES

Across

2 Who did Colin Cooper replace as Boro's first team coach in December 2006? (5, 5)

4 What is the name of the striker who left Boro for Italian side Siena in January 2007? (9)

7 Boro signed two players from Derby County in January 2003. One was Malcolm Christie but who was the other? (7)

10 What is Andrew Taylor's regular position at Boro? (4, 4)

11 Boro played the same team in the last game of 2005-06 and the last game of 2006-07. Which team was it? (6)

13 Boro played AZ Alkmaar in the UEFA Cup in 2005-06. But what country are AZ Alkmaar from? (7)

14 Who is Boro's assistant manager? (6)

18 Winger Adam Johnson spent part of the 2006-07 season on loan to which club? (5, 6)

19 What was the name of Boro's ground before the Riverside Stadium? (8)

20 From what country was former Boro star Alen Boksic? (7)

Down

1 From which club did Boro sign Julio Arca in 2006? (10)

3 Who did Boro sign from Chelsea for £6 million in the summer of 2006? (6, 4)

5 Emanuel Pogatetz is from which country? (7)

6 Was Andrew Davies born in Middlesbrough, Redcar or Stockton? (8)

8 What was the name of Boro's shirt sponsor before 888.com? (4, 1, 5)

9 What is the name of the Boro player who joined Birmingham during the summer of 2007? (7)

12 What was the middle name of former Boro striker Jimmy Hasselbaink? (5)

15 Which Italian team did Boro beat on the way to the 2006 UEFA Cup final? (4)

16 Who was Boro's top scorer last season (2006-07)? (6)

17 How many goals did Micky Burns score in Boro's 7-2 win over Chelsea in 1978? (4)

Answers on page 61

Middlesbrough Football Club 2007/08

Celebrity Boro Fans

Next time you're at the Riverside, take a close look at the fans around you. They just might be famous!

— MARK BENTON

Claim to fame: Star of Nationwide and MFC adverts plus TV shows like Northern Lights and Doctor Who.
Born: Grangetown.
Best ever Boro match: Carling Cup final v Bolton.
All-time fave Boro player: Juninho.
Quote: "The season we got relegated my wife said that I should support another club and get one that wins. She didn't understand that you can't do that!"

KIRSTEN O'BRIEN

Claim to fame: TV presenter for CBBC and Totally Doctor Who.
Born: Nunthorpe.
Best ever Boro match: Carling Cup final, Cardiff.
All-time fave Boro player: Juninho – he was brilliant!
Quote: "I'm constantly telling people about the joys of Middlesbrough and the delights of being a Boro fan!"

MARCUS BENTLEY

Claim to fame: The voice of Big Brother.
Born: Gateshead (but grew up in Stockton).
Best ever Boro match: Basel or Steaua Bucharest UEFA Cup wins.
All-time fave Boro player: David Armstrong.
Quote: "I went to my first match when I was about 12, which is quite old for your first match really. I have just taken my lad to his first match and he is seven."

— PAUL SMITH

Claim to fame: Lead singer of hit band Maximo Park.
Born: Billingham.
Best ever Boro match: beating Steaua Bucharest 4-3 in UEFA Cup semi-final.
All-time fave Boro player: Bernie Slaven.
Quote: "If Maximo Park become big in America, I might help out Steve Gibson and put a few quid in the Boro!"

— ALISTAIR GRIFFIN

Claim to fame: runner-up in TV show Fame Academy.
Born: Castleton.
Best ever Boro match: The UEFA Cup semi-final against Steaua Bucharest.
All-time fave Boro player: Bernie Slaven or John Hendrie.
Quote: "My favourite current Boro player is 'Mad Dog' Emanuel Pogatetz. I just like his spirit, he has a Middlesbrough heart."

— CHRIS TOMLINSON

Claim to fame: British long jump record-holder.
Born: Middlesbrough.
Best ever Boro match: UEFA Cup semi-final against Steaua Bucharest.
All-time fave Boro player: Bernie Slaven.
Quote: "Lee Cattermole is my favourite current Boro player, simply because of his style of play. I like the way he puts himself about and shows grit."

Jonathan Woodgate

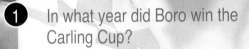

QUIZ 2:
Boro's History

Answers on page 61

1. In what year did Boro win the Carling Cup?

2. Which Portuguese team knocked Boro out of the UEFA Cup in 2004-05?

3. Who did England play in an international match at the Riverside Stadium in 2003?

4. True or false: Mark Schwarzer has played more games for Boro than anyone else in the club's history?

5. Who scored for Boro at Wembley in the 1997 Coca-Cola Cup final against Leicester City?

6. Who was manager of Boro when they moved to the Riverside Stadium in 1995?

Alf Common

7. In what year did Boro move to Ayresome Park? Was it (a) 1903 (b) 1905 (c) 1955?

8. True or false: when Boro bought centre-forward Alf Common in 1905 it was the first time any club had paid a transfer fee of £1,000?

9. From which country was former Boro striker Alen Boksic?

10. In what Dutch city did Boro play Sevilla in the 2006 UEFA Cup final?

10 Greatest Games In

10 **BORO 4 Leeds United 1, Premier League**

August 22 1992

The day newly-promoted Boro destroyed the reigning champions, with former Leeds players John Hendrie and Tommy Wright stars of the show and both adding goals to a double strike from Paul Wilkinson.

9 **Man United 2 BORO 3, Premier League**

December 19 1998

Boro had not won at Old Trafford for more than 60 years so former star striker Bernie Slaven thought there would be no problem when he promised before the game that he would show his backside in Binns' window if Bryan Robson's side took all three points. He lived to regret those words as Hamilton Ricard, Dean Gordon and Brian Deane fired Boro into a three-goal lead.

8 **BORO 2 Bolton 1, Carling Cup final**

February 29 2004

After 128 years in the waiting, Boro grabbed their first major silverware on an emotional afternoon at Cardiff's wonderful Millennium Stadium – and how Teesside celebrated!

Passion-fuelled
Boro raced into a two-goal lead in the opening four minutes through a close-range goal from Joseph-Desire Job and a penalty from Bolo Zenden – then lived on their nerves for the next 86 minutes as Bolton fought their way back into the final.

But the day belonged to Boro and chairman Steve Gibson was lofted onto the shoulders of the players as stars and fans began celebrations that would go on long into the night.

7 **BORO 3 Liverpool 3, Premier League**

August 17 1996

New £7 million signing Fabrizio Ravanelli achieved perhaps the greatest Boro debut ever with a hat-trick as the home side came from behind three times in a truly awesome first game of the season.

6 **BORO 4 Blackpool 0, Division One**

November 22 1947

Cec McCormack scored twice and Micky Fenton and Johnny Spuhler both hit the net – but this game was later remembered as "The Mannion Match" because Boro's England star was simply sensational. Afterwards, the Evening Gazette described Mannion – known as The Golden Boy – as "incomparable" and a "football artist".

5 **BORO 3 Chesterfield 3, FA Cup semi-final**

April 13 1997

Perhaps the greatest FA Cup game of all-time? This was the game that had everything – apart from a Boro victory! Minnows Chesterfield raced into a two-goal lead before 10-man Boro fought back to force extra-time, go in front through defender Gianluca Festa, only to see their Second Division opponents equalise with virtually the last touch of the game. Thankfully, Boro won the replay 3-0.

4 **BORO 2 Liverpool 0, Coca-Cola Cup semi-final 2nd leg**

February 18 1998

A night remembered by Boro fans lucky enough to be there as one of the greatest ever Riverside atmospheres. The Riverside's flag-waving frenzy saw Bryan Robson's First Division team come from 2-1 behind in the first leg to storm into a 3-2 aggregate lead as early as the fourth minute, with Paul Merson scoring from the penalty spot before Italian Marco Branca made a dream start to his Boro career with a debut goal.

Boro's History

3 **BORO 6 Sunderland 0, Division One**

March 28 1936

It's always special when Boro beat their north-east neighbours. It's special too when we beat the reigning champions. So imagine how good it felt to beat title-holders and league leaders Sunderland by SIX goals!

Flying winger Ralph Birkett scored twice for Boro, with his fellow England international George Camsell also finding the net as Boro powered into a five-goal lead before the dismissal of two Sunderland players and a late sixth to complete a truly magnificent Boro performance.

2 **BORO 4 Basel 1, UEFA Cup quarter-final 2nd leg**

April 6 2006

A match that fans rightly claimed was the greatest in Boro's history – for exactly three weeks! Boro made the Swiss roll as Steve McClaren's side fought their way back from three goals down to win in one of the most unbelievable comebacks of all-time.

Trailing 2-0 from the first leg in Switzerland, Boro looked dead and buried when they conceded again after just 22 minutes – but that only served to kick-start a performance of passion, belief and drama.

Mark Viduka began the comeback with goals either side of half-time before strike partner Jimmy Floyd Hasselbaink blasted in a third with 12 minutes remaining. The spectacular comeback was complete in the 90th minute when Massimo Maccarone fired home to send Boro fans into ecstasy.

BORO 4 Steaua Bucharest 2, UEFA Cup semi-final 2nd leg

April 27 2006

This was a night that Boro fans' dreams are made of! For the second time in three weeks, all seemed lost with Boro trailing 3-0 on aggregate – and we all know that lightning doesn't strike twice, don't we? Wrong!

A battling first leg display in Romania had left Boro trailing by just a single goal and on the verge of our first European final. It all went wrong in the first 23 minutes as Boro went two goals behind on the night and three on aggregate. Surely the dream of a small town in a European final was over?

Massimo Maccarone began the fight-back with a low drive before half-time before the inspirational Mark Viduka headed home Stewart Downing's left-wing cross to level the scores on the night. Boro fans started to believe that the impossible could be possible yet again when Chris Riggott levelled the aggregate scores – but still Boro trailed on the away goals rule. Still another goal was needed.

Steaua's wilting defence gave way for a fourth time. Downing beat his marker on the left before swinging in another inch-perfect cross and achieved his third assist of the half as Maccarone powered home a fantastic diving header to send the Riverside into raptures.

Boro were on their way to Eindhoven – and in the words of Boro commentator Alastair Brownlee "Party! Party! Party! Everyone round my house for

Stewart Downing

Did you know there are Boro supporters clubs all around the UK and even the world? Thanks to the official Boro website at www.mfc.co.uk, here's a complete list of Boro fan groups, from New Zealand to New York and from Nigeria to the North Sea!

If none of these are close to you, then why not form a Boro supporters club of your own? For help and advice how to set up your own group of Boro fans contact Sue Gardener, Chairman of Middlesbrough Official Supporters Club, who acts as coordinator for all the other groups around the world. Sue can be contacted on email suem_g@sky.com

MIDDLESBROUGH OFFICIAL SUPPORTERS CLUB

Chairman: Sue Gardener,
Tel. 01642 899412, email suem_g@sky.com or write to: PO Box 803, Thornaby, Stockton-on-Tees, TS19 1EJ.
Membership is £6 per adult and just £2 for those aged under-16.

MIDDLESBROUGH DISABLED SUPPORTERS ASSOCIATION

Chairman: Paddy Cronesberry,
205 Thornaby Road, Thornaby, Stockton-on-Tees, TS17 6LS or telephone 01642 641620.
Membership costs £3 for adults, £2 for senior citizens and just £1 for juniors.

AZERBAIJAN

Contact: Neil Llewellyn
Email: nntl1962@hotmail.co.uk

BRISBANE, AUSTRALIA

Contact: Trevor Harrington
Email: trevor_harrington@hotmail.com
Website: http://www.roosroosroos.com.au/

CANADA BORO SUPPORTERS CLUB

Contact: Jeff Collins
Email: jeffcollins13@hotmail.com

DERBYSHIRE REDS

Membership is free. Call Duncan Haywood on 01246 811244 or email janeduncan.haywood@btinternet.com

DUBAI BORO SUPPORTERS CLUB

Contact: Craig Dean-Dubai
Email: csddean@hotmail.com

GUINEA BORO SUPPORTERS CLUB

Email: mborofcfans_guinea@africamail.cm

KOREAN BORO SUPPORTERS CLUB

Website: site: http://cafe.daum.net/Middlesbrough

MAINLAND EUROPE BORO SUPPORTERS

Contact: Dennis Abbott
Email: dennis.abbott@cor.europa.eu

BORO FANS MALTA

Contact: Ian Graham
Email: igraham98@yahoo.com

MANCHESTER BORO SUPPORTERS

Contact: Rich Crewe
Email: rich.crewe@lycos.com

NEW YORK/NORTH EAST USA: ERIMUS BRANCH

Contact: Jessica Chamberlin
Email: boroyanklass@mac.com

or Matt Green
Email: mgreen75@mac.com

NEW ZEALAND

Colin Pegg-Auckland
Email: boroladuk@slingshot.co.nz

NIGERIA BORO SUPPORTERS CLUB

Contact: Eniola Akinosho
Email: ennyolla@yahoo.com

NORFOLK BORO SUPPORTERS

Contact: Ian Fowler
Email: ifowler922@yahoo.co.uk

NORTH SEA BORO SUPPORTERS CLUB

Contact: Colin Crawford
Email: crawfordcolin@hotmail.com

NORTH WEST BORO SUPPORTERS CLUB

Contact: Gary Warhurst
Email: el_padre@fsmail.net

NORTHERN IRELAND MIDDLESBROUGH SUPPORTERS CLUB

Contact: nimsc@hotmail.co.uk

NORWAY

Contact: Rune Sandvik
Email: runesandvic@hotmail.com
Website: www.klubbinfo.no/boro

SCARBOROUGH

Contact: Craig Close
Email: ccc73@hotmail.co.uk
HQ: The Nelson Pub

SCOTLAND

Contact: Daniel Gray
Email: msscot@hotmail.co.uk

SEDGEFIELD MIDDLESBROUGH SUPPORTERS

Write to Ray Lower, Sedgefield Cricket Club, Station Road, Sedgefield, or ring Dave Pratt on 07811 875105. Membership is £5 and renewal is £1 per year.

SINGAPORE

Chairman: Peter "Shooter" Schott
Secretary: Ariff Ahmad
Email: ariffahmad@mfc-sg.com
Website: www.MFC-SG.com

MIDDLESBROUGH SUPPORTERS SOUTH

Website: www.mss.org.uk. To join or for information contact: Clare Smith, MSS Membership Secretary, 121 Belgrave Road, Walthamstow, London, E17 8QF or email membership@mss.org.uk. Membership is £15 per member plus £2 for every other additional household member.

SWEDEN: BORO VIKINGS

Contact: Lars Aberg, Kumla, Sweden
Website: http://www.borovikings.se/
Email: lasse.aberg@telia.com

THAILAND

Contact: Brian Abbott
Email: boroboy@loxinfo.co.th

WALES BORO SUPPORTERS CLUB

Contact: Mark Richmond
Email: mark_richmond@hotmail.com

YARM REDS

Contact: Andy Wilson on 07816 606514 or via website at www.yarmreds.co.uk.

Down by the Riverside

Impress your mates with these facts 'n' figures about Boro's home, the Riverside Stadium

Middlesbrough Football Club 2007/08

Boro moved to The Riverside Stadium in August 1995 after leaving Ayresome Park, the club's home of the previous 92 years.

The stadium cost £16 million to build, with another £5 million spent on increasing its capacity from 30,000 to 35,100 in 1998.

The Riverside was the biggest stadium built in the UK for 60 years.

The fastest ever goal at the stadium was scored by Boro striker Hamilton Ricard in a 3-1 win over Wimbledon in April 1999. He scored after just 30 seconds!

Craig Hignett scored the first-ever goal at the stadium, sending Boro on their way to that 2-0 win over Chelsea, with Jan-Aage Fjortoft adding a second goal.

The attendance for the first game at the Riverside was 28,826, the biggest crowd for a Boro home game for 14 years.

The ground was originally called the Cellnet Riverside Stadium and then the BT Cellnet Riverside Stadium after the club's then sponsors.

Boro fans voted to call the club's new home The Riverside Stadium. Other choices were Middlehaven Stadium, Teesside Stadium and Erimus Stadium.

Goalkeeper Mark Schwarzer has played more times at the Riverside than any other player.

The first-ever game at the Riverside was a 2-0 Premier League win against Chelsea on August 26 1995.

During the summer of 2003, Boro hosted a European Championships qualifying match between England and Slovakia. In a 2-1 win, Michael Owen scored both goals for England, whose team also included then Boro skipper Gareth Southgate, Wayne Rooney, Steven Gerrard and Frank Lampard.

Come Behind The Scenes

Have you ever been on a guided tour of the Riverside Stadium? If not, then you're missing out on a mega experience. Each tour takes an hour and is TOTALLY COOL! Here's why...

For most Boro fans, the best bit of a Riverside tour is the players' dressing rooms. You can take a seat where your favourite player usually sits when he's getting ready for the big match and imagine what it's like to hear a team talk from Boro boss Gareth Southgate!

Did you know you can also see a replica of the Carling Cup on a stadium tour? The trophy – a replica of the cup Boro won by beating Bolton at the Millennium Stadium in 2004 – is on display in a cabinet at the Riverside.

Alongside the Carling Cup replica are the boots Bolo Zenden wore when he scored the winning penalty in the cup final and the shirt worn by Joseph-Desire Job, who scored Boro's first goal after only two minutes on that great day.

You can also see international shirts and caps won by famous Boro stars of the past and present – like Wilf Mannion, Mark Schwarzer, Gareth Southgate and Boro's all-time top scorer George Camsell.

And you can take a seat in the Boro boardroom where Chairman Steve Gibson makes all the important decisions – like who to sign next!

You can even walk out of the players' tunnel onto the pitch and imagine what it must be like to be a Boro star.

You can take a look inside the away dressing room – and see how small it is compared to Boro's fab facilities – and then walk out of the players' tunnel towards the Riverside pitch.

If you'd like to book on a tour of the Riverside Stadium, the number to call is …

0844 499 6789.

Tours cost just £2 for those aged under-16 and are only £5 for adults. Don't forget to bring your camera!

Word Search Quiz

Find these words in the grid. Words can go horizontally, vertically or diagonally in all eight directions.

Answers on page 61

B	L	I	A	T	E	Z	E	H	A	P	Y	T	S	D	S	S	M	I	O
A	F	O	P	I	A	G	R	B	A	Y	B	L	V	A	G	M	A	D	K
S	M	R	R	S	T	F	O	T	L	M	R	I	Q	S	O	S	A	S	E
U	B	O	R	O	T	D	V	Y	L	I	E	E	V	I	Z	I	R	F	B
P	G	T	I	T	B	E	E	O	M	D	M	Z	S	P	Z	S	C	R	V
P	A	E	V	H	O	C	V	O	A	D	O	Z	O	O	M	S	A	R	E
O	T	O	E	G	U	J	O	E	D	N	N	A	N	G	M	I	M	M	T
R	O	T	S	I	N	G	I	N	G	L	S	R	S	A	F	E	I	A	S
T	E	Z	U	A	N	O	S	F	I	I	A	D	E	T	I	S	D	N	E
E	S	I	O	N	A	A	V	O	S	E	B	S	V	E	N	A	D	N	O
R	A	E	P	T	Y	M	H	O	O	S	C	S	S	T	O	G	L	I	O
S	W	O	O	D	G	A	T	E	N	B	R	A	O	Z	G	S	E	O	V
Q	O	N	G	E	Z	E	I	V	S	O	A	R	U	N	I	E	S	N	L
O	O	M	A	L	I	A	D	I	E	R	E	E	T	O	N	R	B	G	N
A	O	I	T	A	I	R	E	R	I	V	E	R	H	L	G	G	R	O	E
L	Y	N	E	Y	L	R	P	E	Q	R	S	C	G	G	F	T	O	A	L
H	L	R	Z	R	Q	O	O	I	U	O	B	O	A	E	O	S	U	A	E
A	I	O	E	O	I	I	G	E	A	U	U	L	T	E	I	U	G	O	L
A	E	O	I	E	Z	E	A	V	E	G	L	O	E	N	A	A	H	L	H
K	W	N	O	S	W	R	R	I	V	E	R	S	I	D	E	D	H	O	W
I	G	P	S	H	E	V	U	Z	R	H	C	E	R	S	W	O	O	L	T

- [ ] STEVE GIBSON
- [ ] SOUTHGATE
- [ ] WOODGATE
- [ ] SINGING
- [ ] AYRESOME
- [ ] RIVERSIDE
- [ ] ARCA
- [ ] POGATETZ
- [ ] BORO
- [ ] MIDDLESBROUGH
- [ ] MANNION
- [ ] ALIADIERE
- [ ] SUPPORTERS
- [ ] GOAL

spot the difference

Look closely at the pictures below. Can you find all six differences?

Answers on page 61

BORO JUNIOR LIONS
2007-2008

THE BORO JUNIOR LIONS IS THE BEST CLUB FOR THE WORLD'S BEST FANS

MEMBERSHIP PACK

Every member of the club receives a special membership pack containing the following:
- Membership certificate
- Membership card
- Boro Junior lions Frisbee, drawstring bag, water bottle, compass & Fun ball.

BORO MASCOT

Only members have the chance to lead the team out on to the Riverside pitch

JOIN NOW! CALL: 0844 499 6789 or E-mail: borojuniorlions@mfc.co.uk

QUIZ 1:
The Players

1. Real Madrid
2. Ghana
3. Massimo Maccarone
4. Seb Hines
5. Rangers
6. Mark Viduka
7. Stewart Downing
8. Andrew Taylor
9. Emanuel Pogatetz
10. True

QUIZ 2:
Boro's History

1. 2004
2. Sporting Lisbon
3. Slovakia
4. False
5. Fabrizio Ravanelli
6. Bryan Robson
7. 1903
8. True
9. Croatia
10. Eindhoven

Word Search Quiz

B	L	I	A	T	E	Z	E	H	A	P	Y	T	S	D	S	S	M	I	O
A	F	O	P	I	A	G	R	B	A	Y	B	L	V	A	G	M	A	D	K
S	M	R	R	S	T	F	O	T	L	M	R	I	Q	S	O	S	A	S	E
U	B	O	R	O	T	D	V	Y	L	I	E	E	V	I	Z	I	R	F	B
P	G	T	I	T	B	E	E	O	M	D	M	Z	S	P	Z	S	C	R	V
P	A	E	V	H	O	C	V	O	A	D	O	Z	O	O	M	S	A	R	E
O	T	O	E	G	U	J	O	E	D	N	N	A	N	G	M	I	M	M	T
R	O	T	S	I	N	G	I	N	G	L	S	R	S	A	F	E	I	A	S
T	E	Z	U	A	N	O	S	F	I	I	A	D	E	T	I	S	D	N	E
E	S	I	O	N	A	A	V	O	S	E	B	S	V	E	N	A	D	N	O
R	A	E	P	T	Y	M	H	O	O	S	C	S	S	T	O	G	L	I	O
S	W	O	O	D	G	A	T	E	N	B	R	A	O	Z	G	S	E	O	V
Q	O	N	G	E	Z	E	I	V	S	O	A	R	U	N	I	E	S	N	L
O	O	M	A	L	I	A	D	I	E	R	E	E	T	O	N	R	B	G	N
A	O	I	T	A	I	R	E	R	I	V	E	R	H	L	G	G	R	O	E
L	Y	N	E	Y	L	R	P	E	Q	R	S	C	G	G	F	T	O	A	L
H	L	R	Z	R	Q	O	O	I	U	O	B	O	A	E	O	S	U	A	E
A	I	O	E	O	I	I	G	E	A	U	U	L	T	E	I	U	G	O	L
A	E	O	I	E	Z	E	A	V	E	G	L	O	E	N	A	A	H	L	H
K	W	N	O	S	W	R	R	I	V	E	R	S	I	D	E	D	H	O	W
I	G	P	S	H	E	V	U	Z	R	H	C	E	R	S	W	O	O	L	T

Spot the difference

Crossword Quiz

Across

2) STEVE ROUND, 4) MACCARONE, 7) RIGGOTT, 10) LEFT BACK,
11) FULHAM,
13) HOLLAND, 14) CROSBY, 18) LEEDS UNITED, 19) AYRESOME,
20) CROATIA

Down

1) SUNDERLAND, 3) ROBERT HUTH, 5) AUSTRIA, 6) STOCKTON,
8) DIAL A PHONE, 9) PARNABY, 12) FLOYD, 15) ROMA, 16) VIDUKA
17) FOUR